Practical
BONSAI

Colin Lewis

The Crowood Press

First published in 1992 by
The Crowood Press Ltd
Ramsbury, Marlborough
Wiltshire SN8 2HR

© The Crowood Press Ltd 1992

All rights reserved. No part of this publication may be
reproduced or transmitted in any form or by any means,
electronic or mechanical, including photocopy, recording,
or any information storage and retrieval system without
permission in writing from the publishers.

British Library Cataloguing in Publication Data

A catalogue record for this book is available from the British
Library.

ISBN 1 85223 661 2

Acknowledgements

Artwork by Claire Upsdale-Jones.
Photographs by Sue Atkinson and Colin Lewis.

Typeset by Chippendale Type Ltd, Otley, West Yorkshire
Printed and bound in Great Britain by
BPCC Hazell Books, Aylesbury

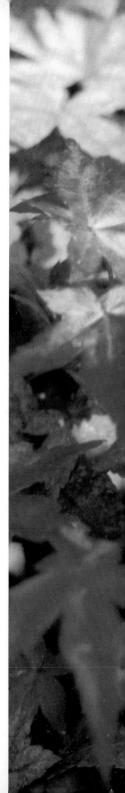

CONTENTS

INTRODUCTION

To many people, bonsai is shrouded in oriental mystique and the successful cultivation of these miniature trees seems far beyond their reach. Yet in essence a bonsai is merely a sophisticated pot plant whose creation and maintenance are based on common horticultural practices. The few techniques specific to bonsai are relatively easy to learn and require no special skills. Once you have mastered these techniques, all you need is a little artistic ability and a fair amount of patience, and as time passes you will be rewarded with many hours of pleasure as your creation matures and, under your control, adopts the form of a full-sized tree.

The first record of the existence of bonsai appeared in temple wall paintings in China during the Han dynasty, 200 years BC. These took the form of potted landscapes complete with trees, rocks and mosses. As the Chinese influence spread throughout the Orient, so did the practice of growing miniature trees in containers. Naturally, when the Chinese invaded Japan in the Middle Ages, the Buddhist monks – who were the custodians of all forms of cultural endeavour – took with them their precious little trees. The Japanese adopted bonsai along with many other aspects of Chinese culture and, true to form, developed and refined it until it became the high art-form it is today.

The Japanese characters which form the word 'bonsai' are identical to the Chinese, although they are now pronounced differently (the Chinese pronunciation is *Punsai*). The characters translate literally as 'potted plant or tree' but the true definition is far more dignified. To qualify as a bonsai the plant must possess all the qualities of a full-sized tree in nature and together with its pot must form an aesthetic entity.

For many years during Japan's feudal past, bonsai were so highly regarded that only those people of high birth were permitted to own them. Since at that time all

Bon – *tree,* sai – *pot or dish.*

bonsai were developed from ancient trees which had been naturally dwarfed on the mountains by the action of wind, snow and landslides, their tenacity and durability gained them a reputation for possessing spiritual qualities above the heads of the masses.

It was not until well into the twentieth century that bonsai culture began to be practised by the ordinary Japanese citizen, and not until after the Second World War that its popularity spread to the West. Nowadays, so great is the demand for ready-made and economically priced bonsai that hundreds of thousands are imported each year from commercial growers in China, Taiwan, Korea and Israel. However, it is sad to say, the vast majority of these plants do not deserve to be called bonsai, they are merely rooted cuttings planted in shallow containers and sold to the gullible public at greatly inflated prices. They are almost all tropical species, which means they need to be grown indoors in this country. Under these conditions, their growth is slowed down or even halted entirely, which renders them impossible to

Satsuki azalea (Rhododendron indicum), *root-over-rock style. The mass of tiny crimson flowers contrast with the tangle of roots clinging tightly to the rock to create a stunning and unusual bonsai.*

train, thereby missing the whole point of growing bonsai.

In this book I will concentrate entirely on hardy species which need to be kept out-doors, where trees *should* live, where they can soak in the sun, the rain and the wind, and will become naturally weathered as the seasons pass.

1 • BONSAI STYLES

As the art of bonsai developed over the centuries, it became desirable to define the various shapes employed. Although these shapes were based on natural tree forms, they had to be simplified because of the reduction in scale. For example the 'formal upright' bonsai, with only a few branches, can evoke images of mighty conifers bearing many branches. In fact, it would not be untrue to say that these definitions describe the tree forms upon which the bonsai are based, rather than the bonsai themselves.

Although in some cases the definitions are quite precise, they should only be used as guidelines since each tree presents its owner with unique possibilities which should not be sacrificed for the sake of conformity. The most important aim is to achieve a result which is pleasing to its creator.

Chokkan – *formal upright style.*

Chokkan (Formal Upright)

This is one of the most difficult styles to achieve because the tree's trunk must be dead straight and taper uniformly from base to tip. The lowest branch should be about one-third of the way up the trunk and to one side, the next a little higher and on the other side, the third higher still but to the rear. This pattern is continued in diminishing proportions to the top. Forward-facing branches should be avoided below the top third of the tree.

Moyogi (Informal Upright)

In contrast with the formal upright style, this is possibly the easiest to achieve and certainly the most common style of bonsai.

The trunk should ideally emerge from the soil at a slight angle and then gently curve in the opposite direction. This 'lazy-S' configuration continues in diminishing proportions to the apex of the tree. The branches

Moyogi – *informal upright style.*

should emerge on the outside of each curve where possible, but *never* on the inside. This would jar the eye and ruin the effect. Forward-facing branches should be avoided on the lower part of the tree in order to expose as much of the trunk shape as possible. Back branches ought to be included in the upper part of the tree to create depth and the top should incline slightly forwards, giving the impression of greater height.

In practice, any tree with a curved trunk and which does not fall happily into any other style will probably be accepted as an informal upright.

Hokidachi – *broom style.*

Hôkidachi (Broom Style)

The most 'tree-like' of all bonsai styles, *Hôkidachi* consists of a short straight trunk bearing at its top an even spreading crown of branches which should ideally all be of similar thickness. These branches divide and sub-divide, forming a pattern of increasingly fine twigs which eventually create an even-domed crown.

Kengai (Cascade)

Shakan – *slanting style.*

Shakan (Slanting Style)

As the name implies, any tree with a fairly straight, slanting trunk and with branches placed similarly to the formal or informal upright styles will qualify as a *Shakan*. However, if the branches all emerge from the side to which the trunk is leaning, the style becomes windswept (*Fukinagashi*).

Fashioned after trees which have had to endure the harshest of mountain conditions, being weighted down by snow and battered by avalanches, this is the most dramatic of all bonsai styles. There are no real rules as such, save that the trunk should bend over the edge of the pot as soon as possible after emerging from the soil and the apex or tip should be below the bottom of the pot. A similar style, *Han-Kengai* or

Kengai – *cascade style.*

semi-cascade, differs insofar as the tip need only fall below the *rim* of the pot.

Han-Kengai – *semi-cascade style.*

Fukinagashi (Windswept Style)

Although the inspiration for this style is obvious, it is by no means easy to achieve a convincing result and high quality *Fukinagashi* bonsai are rare. There are no hard and fast rules in the creation of this style so the imagination can take over, but it is important to keep in mind the tearing action of the wind.

Fukinagashi – *windswept style.*

Bunjingi (Literati Style)

This is the only style inherited from the Chinese and, as the name suggests, was first created by the 'men of letters' in ancient China. The style is based on the calligraphic quality of old Chinese paintings, where a single brush-stroke could suggest an entire tree. For this reason, the trunk of a literati bonsai must be full of character and contain many changes of direction. It is important to have considerable taper from base to apex and to limit the foliage to the uppermost part of the tree. This foliage should be kept to a bare minimum – just enough to keep the tree alive and healthy and in good condition.

Sekijôju – *root-over-rock style.*

Bunjingi – *Literati style.*

Sekijôju (Root-Over-Rock-Style)

Horticulturally, this is a little more tricky to create than other styles and it also takes rather longer. The tree itself may follow any suitable configuration: informal upright, semi or full cascade, windswept etc., but the roots must be tightly wrapped around a rock. The result must appear natural, which is not as easy as it sounds, and must imitate a tree which has grown for many years in a rocky landscape where the surrounding soil has been eroded to expose the roots.

Sôju (Twin-Trunk Style)

There are names for three, five, seven trunks and so on (even numbers are considered unlucky and are difficult to arrange aesthetically), but a description of this one will suffice. Obviously there are two trunks,

Sôju – *twin-trunk style.*

one being shorter and thinner than the other. The trunks may follow any configuration, which often causes the name to be used in conjunction with another, for example twin-trunk windswept. Ideally, the smaller trunk should be planted slightly to the rear of the larger one in order to create perspective.

Kabudachi (Clump Style)

There may be any number of trunks (even numbers under ten excluded), but they must all be connected at the base. This is normally achieved by cutting off a single trunk at ground level and using the many new shoots which emerge from the stump to form new trunks.

Netsunagari (Raft Style)

'A forest from a single tree'. The raft style is a group of any (odd) number of trunks following any configuration, which have been created by laying a single tree on its side in the pot, and training selected branches upwards to form trunks. After a period of time, roots form along the horizontal trunk to give the impression of many trees growing close together. This style, in common with *Kabudachi*, has a horticultural advantage over groups of separate trees since, being all one plant, the different trunks are not competing with each other and there is no risk of the smaller trees being starved by the larger ones.

Netsunagari – *sinuous raft style.*

Yôse-Ue (Group Style)

Any number of trees (again, odd numbers preferred) may be used to create a group or forest planting. In order to create perspective and depth, the smaller trees should be placed towards the rear and the larger ones in front and towards the centre. No three trees should form a straight line and no tree should be obscured from view by another

Kabudachi – *clump style.*

Ezo spruce (Picea jezoensis), group planting. All the magic and mystery of the darkest forest are evoked by this skilful arangement of trees of widely differing ages. Note also the broom-style Japanese hornbeam in the background.

when the composition is seen from the front. Often, it is possible to create delightful and very realistic forests in a short time by using young spindly seedlings which would be of very little value in any other style. The group can be added to over the years as new seedlings or cuttings become available.

This is by no means a complete list of bonsai styles, but those not mentioned are uncommon and more obscure in their definitions.

As a footnote to this chapter, I would suggest that you learn by all means the various styles and their definitions, but please do not allow them to dictate to you. When you come to style your own bonsai, consider the tree first. The tree will tell you what style suits it best and it would be wrong to force it into any other. Once you have completed the design, you can then see what category it falls into and make any fine adjustments later.

Yôse-Ue – *group style.*

2 • TOOLS AND EQUIPMENT

There is a large number of specialist tools available from bonsai nurseries, almost all made in Japan and of a very high quality. There is no doubt that they make the job a lot easier, but that does not necessarily mean that you will achieve better results with them than you would with tools you already have around the home. So, to begin with, save your money for plants and pots and invest in special tools one by one, as you become more committed to the hobby.

Basic Tools

First, you will need a good pair of seca-teurs – the bypass type, *not* the anvil type – for cutting twigs and branches. Use a new-ish pair which are still sharp at the tip. Next, you will need a **sharp modelling knife or scalpel** for cleaning up pruning scars and carving dead wood. A Stanley knife is no good because the handle and blade are far too bulky for use in the confined spaces between bonsai branches.

You may find a **small saw** useful for tackling thicker branches and roots. Japanese saws cut on the pull-stroke as opposed

A broom style Stewartia. *This species is popular in Japan because of its orange-red bark and fine twigs.*

A selection of Japanese tools and wire. The tools include branch cutters, wire cutters, shears, pliers and tweezers.

to the push-stroke, which is ideal since it minimizes the risk of buckling the blade and provides a greater degree of control. However, a keyhole saw or coarse fretsaw blade will do.

You will need two kinds of **scissors**, both very sharp. First, a pair of medium-sized household scissors which are firmly assembled and whose two halves do not wobble. If they are loosely assembled, you will find that they will not cut cleanly and strips of bark will get caught between the blades as they pass each other, causing considerable frustration. Second, a pair of nail scissors will be invaluable. They must be new enough to cut right up to the tips of the blades, which should be pointed. If you can find a pair with curved blades, so much the better. In fact, I still use nail scissors for intricate work in spite of the fact that I have a drawer full of Japanese tools.

A good pair of long tweezers may come in useful. Eyebrow tweezers are no use because they are far too short and the ends never seem to meet accurately. Next, wire cutters. You may find that you will need two sizes: a fairly hefty pair for thick wire and a small, instrument maker's pair for the fine stuff. As with all cutting tools, it is essential that they cut right up to the tips. This is because you will also want to use them for cutting wire off the tree – much easier and safer than trying to unwind it.

Two types of pliers will be invaluable. A pair of long-nosed electrical pliers and a small pair of the round-nosed type. The usefulness of the former is obvious; the latter comes in very handy for fashioning the initial hook or partial spiral for anchoring the wire prior to coiling it around the branch.

If you can find one, an old turntable of some kind is useful. There is nothing more tiresome than having to heave heavy pots around or get up and lean over the plant to work on the other side. An old record player or even a discarded office chair can easily be adapted.

Wire

Commercial nurseries sell Japanese aluminium wire and would have you believe that it is the only wire to use. In fact, in Japan, aluminium wire is only used on deciduous trees and copper wire is used on all conifers. Copper can equally well be used on deciduous trees provided that you are careful not to use wire which is too thick and strong for the job in hand.

Alternatively, you can use plastic-coated iron wire which is sold in garden centres and comes in two thicknesses. The thickest is quite stiff and will only be of use on the heavier branches but the thinner wire is ideal as a general purpose wire. It is also possible to buy aluminium horticultural wire, but it is fairly weak and of little use.

For many years I used copper almost exclusively. It was not until I visited Japan to attend the first World Bonsai Convention and managed to pick up a suitcase full of aluminium wire at a very cheap price that my habits changed. When that runs out I will revert to copper. Even so, for very fine work I still use copper wire since its greater holding power means I can get away with a thinner gauge, making it easier to apply.

Copper wire is easy to acquire, electrical cable and telephone wires being the prime sources. With a little persuasion it is possible to build a collection of copper wire ranging from 2.5mm thick right down to 0.25mm. The plastic can be burnt off, and allowing the wire to cool slowly tempers it. In some instances, especially with the thicker wires, you may wish to leave the plastic coating intact to act as a cushion and to minimize the risk of damaging the bark.

wood

old office chair stand

How to construct a turntable from an old office chair.

Now you have everything you need to create a bonsai – except, that is, for the plant.

3 • THE RAW MATERIAL

In theory, any tree, shrub or other woody plant can be grown as a bonsai. In practice it's not quite that simple. To start with, some species react badly to root disturbance; others simply dislike living in pots. But the most important consideration is the size of leaf. It is quite easy to reduce the leaf size of any plant by constant pruning of new growth, but there is a limit to just how far you can go. A horse-chestnut leaf, even at a quarter of its full size, would look out of place on all but the largest bonsai.

There are three main ways of obtaining suitable plants: by propagation – seeds, cuttings, layering; by buying container-grown plants at garden centres, or by collecting from open ground – your garden or, with consent, other people's land. Most bonsai enthusiasts use a combination of all three. The main factors which should influence your choice of method will be availability, economy and the desired finished size of your bonsai. For example, Japanese maples are expensive to buy and impossible to find in open ground, but seeds are readily available from a number of sources. Also, if you fancy growing a three-foot tall bonsai, forget seeds and cuttings unless you are prepared to let the plant grow in the ground for a number of years before starting work.

Garden Centre Plants

Garden centres and nurseries provide a ready source of excellent raw material for converting to bonsai. However, before you buy there are a few points to bear in mind.

First, make sure the species or variety is suitable for bonsai. Don't be taken in by the twisted branch structure of the contorted willow (*Salix matsudana* 'Tortuosa') or the delicate winter flowers of *Viburnum × bodnantense*. Neither respond well to the sort of pruning involved, either above or below ground.

Ensure that the plant is established in its pot. The presence of moss and weed seedlings on the surface of the compost is a good indication that the plant has not been recently repotted. Never buy bare-rooted plants. Buy in the growing season if possible. This will enable you to judge the vigour of the plant and will avoid any disappointments when deciduous species bought in the dormant season fail to come into leaf in spring.

Pay careful attention to the size of the plant you buy. Remember that you will be reducing it drastically. A few years ago I bought a 10ft (3m) tall hornbeam (*Carpinus betula*) and within three seasons converted it to a 2½ft (80cm) tall bonsai. On the other hand, if you locate a species you particularly

Hornbeam – *Carpinus betulus* (Native)
Sources Seed takes two or three years to germinate and cuttings are slow to establish. By far the best source is garden centres where hedging stock or even larger trees intended for large gardens or parks may be bought.
The leaves of hornbeam are similar to those of beech but are slightly more pointed and have a serrated edge. The trunk of a mature tree becomes fluted and this feature is often evident in much younger specimens.

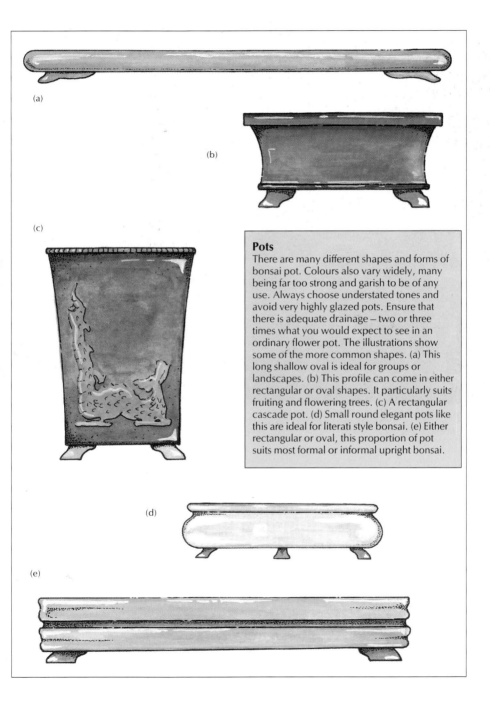

(a)

(b)

(c)

Pots

There are many different shapes and forms of bonsai pot. Colours also vary widely, many being far too strong and garish to be of any use. Always choose understated tones and avoid very highly glazed pots. Ensure that there is adequate drainage – two or three times what you would expect to see in an ordinary flower pot. The illustrations show some of the more common shapes. (a) This long shallow oval is ideal for groups or landscapes. (b) This profile can come in either rectangular or oval shapes. It particularly suits fruiting and flowering trees. (c) A rectangular cascade pot. (d) Small round elegant pots like this are ideal for literati style bonsai. (e) Either rectangular or oval, this proportion of pot suits most formal or informal upright bonsai.

(d)

(e)

All previous year's shoots should be shortened to one to three buds in order to promote a fine network of twigs.

fancy, but the example is too small, buy it anyway and allow it to grow on in open ground for a few years.

Choosing the Plant

You can always spot bonsai enthusiasts in a garden centre. They are the ones crawling around on hands and knees poking about in the pots; first checking one, then another, then back again. This is because the most important features to look for are an interesting trunk shape with good taper potential and a well structured surface-root pattern. These 'surface roots' will no doubt

be below the surface in the pot so a little gentle scratching away of compost will be necessary.

It is always possible to grow on new branches or to alter the shapes and positions of existing ones, but once the trunk and surface roots have become established, they are there for ever.

Next try to look for the 'bonsai within' (*see* page 11). It takes a little practice, but before long you will become quite skilled at on-the-spot analysis of the possibilities. Try to visualize the different trunk lines and branch placements. Don't expect to make firm decisions at this point, just satisfy your

GOOD ROOTS   BAD ROOTS

When choosing the plant, look for a well-structured surface root pattern.

mind that there are several good options open to you.

When you get your treasured plant home, resist the temptation to work on it straight away. Live with it for a few days or weeks and you will be surprised at how many more alternative designs you detect. I usually buy several plants at once and always keep a stand-by stock of eight or ten waiting to be worked on. This way I avoid the frustration of not having raw material when the mood takes me and I can work a bit at a time on several plants at once, thereby reducing the shock to any one plant and minimizing the risk of over-hasty decisions.

One final point: don't forget to water and feed the raw material regularly to achieve the best results.

Collecting From Open Ground

This can be a contentious topic since in Japan and to a certain extent in this country too, the finest material for bonsai is found growing in mountainous areas where its struggle for survival against harsh elements keeps it small and imparts much character to the trunk and branches.

In the UK, it is illegal to remove any plant from the wild, so don't do it. Having said that, many farmers and landowners will allow you to remove stunted or damaged trees from their land if you ask (and you *must* ask), especially if they are in danger of blocking ditches or are in hedgerows which are scheduled to be grubbed up.

Roadside verges, neglected municipal land, gardens of about-to-be-demolished houses and even the neglected corners of your own or your neighbour's garden are also excellent sites for finding suitable plants. I must stress again that you *must* get permission before collecting from other people's land.

Characteristics

The characteristics you need to look for are similar to those in garden centre plants, but you will need to have a little more imagination. Don't waste your time looking for the perfect natural bonsai – it doesn't exist! Nature does not carefully place each branch and twig in order to create a perfect replica of a full-grown tree. What nature does do, however, is to present you with a trunk with all kinds of features: scars, twists, contortions, etc., which no human mind could conceive and no human hand could achieve. It will be up to you to build the rest of the tree on to this basic trunk, keeping it in character and balance with what nature has done before you.

Next time you get the chance, have a look at the shrubs in your garden. Look at the base of your cotoneaster or pyracantha. Or perhaps you have a self-sown hawthorn or pine which has been growing by the garage door and gets damaged each time it is opened. Maybe there is something which

gets its top cut off each time you mow the lawn, or what about that dusty old privet hedge you have been dying to get rid of for years? All these things provide superb opportunities for bonsai. Your garden holds a wealth of possibilities if you look carefully and with bonsai in mind.

Lifting the Plant

If you are collecting from a garden or from good loamy soil, you should be able to lift the plant in one go. In early spring dig a trench around the plant about 8in (20cm) away from the trunk and one spade deep. Then undercut the plant and lift. Take care not to damage too many of the fine roots or your own back!

Since you will have reduced the root mass considerably you should also reduce the

'Before and after'. (a) The collected tree is showing potential (the shaded area is the bit we need). (b) New branches grown on from edges of pruning wounds.

top growth in a similar proportion. It is tempting to carry out an instant design at this stage but rushed decisions are seldom the best ones, so resist that temptation. Shorten all the really heavy trunks and branches but be sure to leave sufficient buds or foliage to nourish the roots. The time to make structural changes by pruning will come later when you have had plenty of time to contemplate all the options at your leisure.

Use a hose to wash away all the soil and assess the root structure. If there are sufficient fine feeder roots growing from the base of the trunk, you can cut back as many of the thick roots as you dare. Make the cuts a few inches away from the trunk and angle them as shown in the diagram. If there are no feeder roots you should clean up the wounds on the existing roots with your

secateurs without shortening them any further.

New feeder roots can be encouraged to grow by cutting away strips of bark from

Cut the thick roots back hard, provided that there are sufficient fine feeder roots at the base of the trunk.

Hawthorn – *Crataegus monogyna* (Native)
Sources Seedlings abound in the vicinity of older trees. Good plants can be bought as hedging stock in garden centres but the finest opportunities are to be found in condemned hedgerows. Hawthorns need a great deal of care when digging them up from open ground so the landowner's permission and co-operation must always be obtained.

Small, three-lobed leaves borne on reddish shoots, masses of white, pink or even double pink flowers and red fruits in autumn make hawthorn possibly the best of our native flowering trees for bonsai.

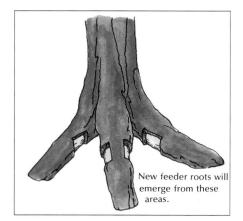

New feeder roots will emerge from these areas.

Cutting away strips of bark from around the trunk base and on the underside of the thick roots will encourage new feeder roots to develop.

Azalea – *Rhododendron indicum* spp. (Japan)
Sources   Available in most garden centres or can be grown from cuttings. There are many potentially superb bonsai growing in gardens which will respond favourably to being dug up in spring as soon as the flowers have passed.

Small semi-evergreen leaves, compact growth and a profusion of small flowers borne in May make this the supreme species for flowering bonsai. Flowers range from white through all shades of pink, red, purple and blue.

beginning to train it. It has suffered a shock and needs to recover and create a new system of fibrous roots before it is strong enough to respond favourably to your attentions. You can keep the growth under control by light pruning during this time but don't overdo it. The plant needs foliage to nourish the new roots every bit as much as it needs new roots to nourish the foliage.

Water and feed regularly using a half strength solution for the first season and full strength thereafter.

If you are collecting from poor stony soil or from waterlogged conditions, do the job in three stages, all in early spring. First, dig a trench half-way round the tree, about 8in (20cm) from the trunk and one spade deep. Cut cleanly through all the roots within the trench and backfill with the sandy compost mix. You can carry out some pruning of top growth at this time, but only a limited amount.

around the trunk base and on the undersides of the thick roots close to the trunk (*see* illustration).

Planting

Without delay, plant your new acquisition in a large shallow container such as a wooden seed tray or, ideally, a plastic washing-up bowl with five or six 1in (25mm) holes cut in the bottom for drainage. (A piece of hot metal pipe is useful for this purpose.)

You can use standard bonsai compost (*see* page 36) if you wish, but the addition of extra grit or horticultural sharp sand will encourage better and more fibrous root growth. Tie the tree firmly in place with string or wire. Allow the tree to establish for at least a year, maybe two or three, before

Some basic pruning can take place at this time.

Dig a trench half-way around the trunk.

Cut all roots cleanly.

Collecting material from poor, stony soil.

During the following growing season new fibrous roots will grow into the compost-filled trench. If you can, add a little fertilizer to the compost from time to time to encourage the roots to remain in that area. The following spring, repeat the operation on the remaining half of the tree. While you are about it you can carefully excavate a small section of the first trench to check on the root growth. You may risk damaging some of the new roots but the temptation is likely to be impossible to resist.

In the third spring you should be able to lift the entire plant, together with its new mass of roots. From here on, the procedure is the same as for trees lifted at one attempt.

Aftercare

All collected trees should be kept in shaded, humid conditions for a few months to minimize the demand on the roots. The ideal conditions can be created in a polythene greenhouse which has a door at each end and is afforded shade for most of the day. Most serious bonsai enthusiasts treat themselves to a polythene greenhouse or 'polytunnel' sooner or later since it is the perfect plant 'hospital' and is also useful for overwintering slightly tender species.

By mid-summer you should be able gradually to introduce the tree to the open air but still keeping it out of the midday sun

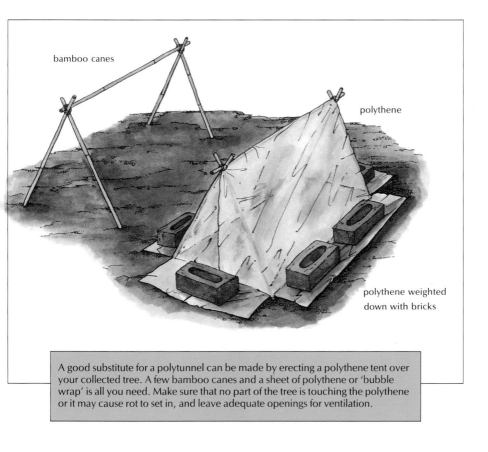

bamboo canes

polythene

polythene weighted down with bricks

A good substitute for a polytunnel can be made by erecting a polythene tent over your collected tree. A few bamboo canes and a sheet of polythene or 'bubble wrap' is all you need. Make sure that no part of the tree is touching the polythene or it may cause rot to set in, and leave adequate openings for ventilation.

A collected spruce (Picea sitchensis), which was rescued from a roadside verge. It has been growing in this training box for two years. (Below) The same spruce after initial styling. The top portion of the trunk has been removed entirely and a shari has been created by stripping the bark from one side. See how some of the roots have also been exposed and stripped of their bark.

until it is obviously growing vigorously. In the second year you can expose it to full sun.

Suitable Species

There are several requirements a plant must fulfil in order for it to be considered suitable for bonsai. Most importantly, it must be able to produce the fine feeder roots which will enable it to live for a great many years in the confines of a pot. These roots must also tolerate pruning and regenerate quickly.

The leaves should either be naturally small or should readily reduce in size under bonsai treatment. The internodes (distances between the leaves on the shoot) should be short and regular.

Finally, the plant must be able to thrive happily in the environment you can offer it, whether this is the garden, the conservatory or the bathroom windowsill. Since we are concentrating on hardy, or so-called out-door trees, the following list does not include any species which would not tolerate a reasonably hard British winter.

Broad-Leaved Trees

Alder   The alder prefers permanently damp conditions and will even live in waterlogged soil and should never be allowed to dry out. It is a vigorous grower, so watch the wiring in case it begins to cut into the rapidly thickening bark. Prune and pinch new growth frequently. Because of its vigour, alder is best suited to bonsai 1ft (30cm) or more tall, although I have seen a few merit-worthy specimens a good deal smaller than that.

Azaleas   These tend to be brittle, so wiring should be carried out only on young growth. Older wood can be carved and hollowed with no ill effect on the tree's health. Azaleas prefer semi-shaded and damp conditions. The roots should never be allowed to dry out but must not become waterlogged. Prune as soon as the flowers have passed.

Beech   The slow-growing habit of beech means that you will achieve better results if you start with a plant which is already several years old. Normal bonsai soil with a little lime added and a sheltered position will suit this tree best. Its coarseness of growth makes it unsatisfactory for bonsai much less than 15in (38cm) tall.

Birch   This is the first tree to colonize vacant ground, so it is accustomed to full sun but it reacts badly to dry roots. At the first hint of drought the fine shoots will die back, even entire branches may be lost, so

Birch – *Betula pendula, B. pubescens* (Native)
Sources   Seedlings grow like grass anywhere within a hundred yards of the nearest birch, so there is never a shortage of opportunity.

Neat, almost triangular leaves are borne on unfortunately long stalks (petioles). The fine reddish shoots which become covered in tiny white specks can form an attractive winter feature.

take extra care. Wire applied in early spring can be removed by June when all but the heaviest of branches will have set. Do not prune until the buds have begun to open in spring, by which time you will be able to see if any branches or shoots have suffered winter die-back. Avoid late summer growth by reducing high nitrogen feed from June onwards.

Cotoneaster Supple branches, small flowers and fruit and extremely compact growth means that wiring can be carried out on a very small scale to produce wonderful shohin or miniature bonsai. Once the main branches have set in position, the rest of the design can be completed by pruning alone. Watch out for adventitious shoots which may spring out from almost anywhere and will grow away rapidly if not cut off. Keep thinning out older wood at the extremities to allow new growth to replace it from further back down the branch. Prune at any time except deep winter.

Elms The roots of elms are slightly fleshy so they prefer not to be constantly frozen and thawed day after day in winter. Long periods of sub-zero temperatures are less harmful. Apart from that, all elms are almost trouble-free. They respond well to root pruning and bud back profusely when branches are pruned. Branches wired in late winter, before the buds have swollen, will set in position by mid-June when the wire should be removed. New growth should be cut back to one or two leaves as soon as it has ripened. Prune in late winter/early spring, or even in August, provided you seal the wounds well to prevent 'bleeding'.

Hawthorn These are tough and extremely resilient and will rebound from a lot of rough treatment with surprising vigour. However, older plants collected from open ground will require at least three or four years to establish themselves before they

Elms – *Ulmus* spp. (Native) *U. parvifolia* (China)
Sources The Chinese elm, *U. parvifolia*, is rare in garden centres but common in bonsai nurseries. It is easily propagated by cuttings, root cuttings or seeds. All other native elms are still quite common in hedgerows and waste land, where suckers or cuttings may be taken with the landowner's permission.
  Small oval leaves with a coarse bristly upper surface and a grey, smooth bark which becomes deeply fissured with age. The leaves of Chinese elm are smaller than other species and are produced at more regular intervals along the shoot.

can be styled, as the roots on such older plants are slow to regenerate. Wood up to ¼in (6mm) thick can be shaped with wire easily, but anything thicker will start to become brittle so care must be taken.

The resilience of hawthorn makes it an ideal species for the beginner, but don't expect flowers to appear on trees which have spent all their lives in pots. Flowers will only appear on a bonsai hawthorn if it was originally styled from a plant which

This Satsuki azalea (Rhododendron indicum) is impossible to age accurately. It would have been collected from the mountains of Japan many generations ago. The trunk base is over 1ft (30cm) thick.

Rhododendron indicum

皐　月　大盃　和長方
492　南国支部　西原　長門

was already mature, or if the seedling or semi-trained bonsai has been allowed to grow unchecked in the ground for a number of years.

Hornbeam Like beech, hornbeam are slow growers so it is best to start with older stock. Wired branches take a little longer to set even though they can thicken quite rapidly, particularly at the top of the tree. Keep a careful eye on the wire and replace it when necessary. Hornbeams suffer badly from leaf-scorch, caused either by hot sun or, more often, by drying winds so keep them in a light but sheltered position.

Japanese quince This tree has the habit of producing lots of suckers – shoots arising from the base of the trunk or from thicker roots. This can be an annoying feature if you are trying to grow a style to which the subject is not suited. However, the beautiful spring flowers on leafless branches make it worthwhile trying to find a style which does work. A little-used style often referred to as the 'octopus' works best. This is really a multi-trunked clump style which has a large number of very short and angular trunks with sparse branches. The shape is achieved entirely by pruning hard back after each flowering period, and again later in the year when next year's flower buds can be detected at the bases of the shoots and back on older wood. This pruning pattern means that for much of the growing season the plant does not look its best – but the spring flowers are worth the wait.

Maples These have opposite foliage which causes the branches to grow in a more angular fashion than alternate-leaved species such as elm. They can be brittle when older, so wiring on wood over two years old should be executed with the utmost care. Branches set in position quickly, and pruning at any time of the year will result in a profusion of new shoots. Keep in semi-shade and well away from drying winds which will cause the leaves to scorch and turn brown at the margins.

The 'octopus' style, though little used, is effective for the Japanese quince.

Maples – *Acer palmatum, A. japonicum* (Japan), *Acer campestris* (Native)
Sources The native field maple is easily grown from seed or may be found as hedging stock in garden centres. The Japanese species are available in garden centres or bonsai nurseries – at a price. However, they will all grow from seed which can be bought from specialist seed merchants.

The very delicate lobed leaves and stunning autumn coloration of the Japanese maples make them a favourite for bonsai of all sizes. On the other hand, the native field maple has a much coarser growth and limits its autumn tones to shades of yellow. Nevertheless, it still makes a fine bonsai.

Pyracantha The clusters of flowers and fruit are so prolific that they often need to be thinned out in order not to strain the tree too much. The young branches are easily wired but wood over three years old can become very hard and impossible to shape. Pyracantha responds well to root pruning and carving and can be cut back very hard from time to time to regenerate young shoots. Normal pruning should take place once the fruit has set and a balance can be achieved between the fruit you want to retain and the new growth you wish to encourage for next year. Old garden shrubs can be cut back to a stump when they are dug up in early spring and new branches can be grown on quickly. The stump can be refined by carving interesting sharis and jins. Keep in full sun.

Willow The first requirement of willow is that it should never be allowed to dry out, even partially. This will inevitably result in die back or even death. Secondly, they will need to be root-pruned at least once every year. Because of their growth rate and leaf size, you should aim at a final size of at least 15in (38cm) tall and a style which follows the natural habit of the tree. *S. babylonica* can be encouraged to weep by tying the young growth down to the trunk for a month or so without any pruning. When they have set in position, the ties are removed and the growth can be pruned back by about a half. These weeping branches will need to be cut away and replaced by new ones every few years.

Try creating a pollard with *S. fragilis* (crack willow). Take a short, thick rooted cutting and allow unrestricted growth from the top for one season. Then cut this back, leaving only a short stub. From then on, all you have to do is prune all new growth back to its base each February, and again around early June. This will reward you with a mass of long, thin, orange-red shoots for winter viewing. Over the years a knotted,

Two Styles for the Willow

S. babylonica can be encouraged to weep by tying down the young growth to the trunk for a month or so without any pruning. When they have set in position, the ties are removed and the growth can be pruned back. These weeping branches will need to be cut away and replaced by new ones every few years.

Try creating a pollard with *S. fragilis* (crack willow). Take a short, thick rooted cutting and allow unrestricted growth from the top for one season. Then cut this back, leaving only a short stub. From then on, all you have to do is prune back all new growth to its base each February, and again around early June. This will reward you with a mass of long, thin, orange-red shoots for winter viewing. Over the years a knotted, gnarled head will develop to the trunk, creating a very authentic appearance.

S. babylonica

shoots are tied in to train them downwards

pollarded willow

gnarled head will develop to the trunk, creating a very authentic appearance.

Zelkova Broom style zelkovas are traditionally created by cutting through a trunk of desired thickness and then cutting an uneven 'V' in the top of the stump. A host of new shoots will emerge from all around the wound and these should be tied tightly together to form a 'shaving brush' effect for at least a year. This ensures that in years to come the transition from trunk to new

(a) Create a short trunk by cutting through a taller trunk in spring and forming an uneven 'V'.

(b) A mass of new shoots will emerge from around the cut surface.

(c) Bind the shoots tightly with tape or raffia to create a smooth transition from trunk to branch.

(d) After a few years of regular clipping, a fine tracery of twigs can be developed.

Creating a broom style zelkova.

branches will be gentle and natural looking rather than harsh and angular. From then on a regime of summer pinching and late winter pruning back to two or three buds will satisfy most training requirements. The occasional thinning out and application of wire will see to the rest.

Conifers

Cryptomeria A well drained soil and full sun for most of the day will suit this species best. Wiring can be done at any time, but watch for signs of cracking where the branch being wired meets the trunk. Also, older branches can become brittle. Hard pruning and constant pinching with the occasional thinning out will rapidly produce well defined and mature foliage pads.

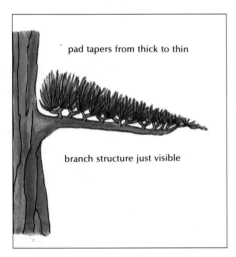

pad tapers from thick to thin

branch structure just visible

Ideal, well defined and mature foliage pads.

Cut away all young adventitious shoots as they appear on old wood in order to keep the branch line clean.

Fir If you are growing a bonsai fir, aim for a tall tree of at least 24in (60cm): this species does not bud back as prolifically as others, so it is not possible to build a small-scale branch structure. You should also wait until the raw material is several years old before potting it up, as root disturbance on young trees drastically reduces vigour.

Hemlock These are fairly slow growing trees when grown in pots, both above and below ground. This means that they will not need to be repotted as frequently as some, and are best converted to bonsai from larger stock. If you prefer to grow your trees from seed, then aim for a small or very small (mame) bonsai. When pruning back long branches to a more suitable length, ensure that you leave sufficient foliage to support the branch. If a branch is cut back too far and all or most of the foliage is removed, it may well die back completely.

Juniper (needle foliage) The most common form of needle juniper bonsai is one which is covered in jins and sharis, making the most of its natural tendency to shed bark from the trunk as branches die off. Junipers will accept major root disturbance provided they have a good pad of fine roots to begin with, but wild plants may need several years to establish before they are strong enough to be worked on. In order to maintain a clean branch line and tight foliage pads, constant pinching is required throughout the summer. Every second or third year you need to thin out some of the tightly packed foliage to let the remaining leaves 'breathe'.

Juniper (cord-like foliage) This must be the easiest of all species to grow as a bonsai. It can be wired, pruned and repotted at any time of year except in the dead of winter provided it is placed in a polytunnel until new growth starts. It is vigorous enough to produce plump foliage pads within a short time, yet will not bolt away if neglected for a while. Even a newly styled tree can appear quite mature.

Juniper (Needle Foliage) – *Juniperus communis, J. rigida* (Europe, Japan)
Sources   Varieties of *J. communis*, many of them dwarf, are common in garden centres. *J. rigida* is available (at a price) from bonsai nurseries. Cuttings are difficult.

Like cryptomeria, needle junipers bud back readily from any wood which still bears some foliage. The term 'needle' is aptly used for they are very sharp and demand an even temper when wiring! In the wild, junipers seldom grow more than 12 or 15ft (3.5 or 4.5m) tall but they produce the most fantastic shaped trunks quite naturally which gives them the appearance of great age.

Juniper (Cord-like Foliage) – *Juniperus chinensis, J. media* (China, Japan)
Sources   Cuttings taken in summer will root easily in a propagator. Garden centres are full of these junipers and some are available in bonsai nurseries.

Seldom more than a large spreading bush, the rich green or blue-green foliage and the reddish bark of Chinese junipers are striking. Like needle junipers, wild plants will often form natural jins and sharis.

A note of caution: Chinese junipers will produce a juvenile 'needle' type foliage after really heavy pruning or root pruning, or as a result of too much fertilizer. While this will eventually settle into adult foliage it can take some years, so it is best to try to avoid it in the first place by being restrained in your treatment. Wire may be needed to hold branches in position for many years before they finally set.

Larch   These are fun to grow as bonsai. They grow quickly enough for their branches to set with wiring within a matter of a few weeks and they respond well to branch and root pruning. When pruning, note where the buds have formed along the branch and cut back to one facing in the direction you want the new growth to take. Rub away any

Rub away any downward-facing buds as soon as they form.

downwards-facing buds as soon as they form.

Pines There are so many varieties of pine that the choice can seem bewildering. Avoid the exotics with long needles and coarse growth. The dwarf varieties such as mugo pine can produce good bonsai but are sometimes disappointing and temperamental. By far the best choice is one of the compact growing varieties of our native scots pine, *Pinus sylvestris*, such as *'nana'* or *'beauvronensis'*. Wire and prune any time from March to September and remove old needles as you go. Repot every two or three years. Pines will tolerate wet or dryish conditions but will only produce small neat needles if kept just moist and no more once the new needles have emerged. Pines will bud back on old wood if healthy and vigorous, but are disappointing if grown in soggy, undernourished soil. Add an extra couple of handfuls of grit or sand to the soil mix.

When designing your pine bonsai look carefully at the full-grown pines in your locality for inspiration. Note the way the branches tend to cascade from the trunk and turn up at the tips so the new active foliage receives full sun. Try to emulate this in your bonsai.

Spruce Quite severe root pruning causes little or no ill effect and the plant soon repays you with renewed vigour. When pruning top growth, seal the wounds immediately to prevent excessive bleeding. Pinch back all new shoots to about a quarter of their length while they are still soft. Every four years you will need to thin out old growth to make room for the new.

Yew Because they are so slow growing it is better to create your yew bonsai from as large a plant as possible, preferably a specimen plant from a garden centre as opposed to a hedging plant, which is less likely to have such a well-formed trunk base. Yew will throw out buds and shoots from very old wood so you can prune away to your heart's content. However, wire will need to stay on for many years before the branches will set, being replaced as the need arises. New shoots on established bonsai should be cut back to three or four pairs of leaves to keep the foliage pads neat.

The vigorous roots of yew are quite thick and fleshy, so they need plenty of room to develop sufficiently to keep the tree healthy. Choose a deepish pot and make sure you use an open soil mix.

When designing your pine bonsai, look carefully at the full-grown pines in your locality for inspiration. Note the way the branches tend to cascade from the trunk and turn up at the tips so the new active foliage receives full sun. Try to emulate this in your bonsai.

4 • BASIC TECHNIQUES

Whatever the origin or size of your chosen plant, the techniques you will need to employ are the same. Always bear in mind that the aim is to create the image of a fully-grown tree in miniature, not just an unnaturally twisted and contorted shape. And remember that all these techniques have been developed over the centuries to work *with* nature, not against it. If these techniques are executed with care the tree will respond well and will live a long and happy life.

Spruce – *Picea* spp. (Widely distributed)
Sources Seedlings, cuttings; garden centres stock many dwarf varieties.
　　Full size varieties of spruce such as Sitka spruce, can make good bonsai if grown as large specimens of at least 24in (60cm). However, their awkward growth pattern makes them quite a challenge and they are not recommended for the novice. On the other hand, most of the many dwarf garden varieties will readily convert to bonsai. Their short, densely packed needles and very short shoots enable a mature looking bonsai to be achieved in a matter of a few years by pruning alone.

This hornbeam (Carpinus betua) *was bought from a garden centre and was originally 9ft (2.7m) tall. The trunk was shortened and a new leader was wired in immediately. After three years, this is the result.*

Repotting and Root Pruning

This is always the most frightening task for the beginner, but it is essential to the plant's health. The periodical pruning of older roots enables the tree to regenerate and prevents it from becoming root-bound in its pot. Early spring is the best time for this.

(a) First, gently remove the tree from the pot. If you see a mass of roots winding around the outside of the soil ball, the tree is due for root pruning. (b) Using a pencil or wire hook or similar, gently tease these long roots away from the rootball until they hang loose. Then begin to comb away the remaining soil from around the edges. Use long strokes working from the middle outwards all around the tree and pay special attention to the underside of the rootball. (c) Having removed about half the soil, the roots are ready for trimming.

(d) Next, cut out all the really thick roots as far back as you can, but take care not to cut off all the fine roots in the process. These fine roots are the ones the tree uses for feeding so you should remove only about half of them. Do this by trimming them neatly with sharp scissors. A healthy tree should have enough fine feeder roots to enable you to trim them back to an inch or so less than the internal dimensions of the pot.

(e) When you have cleaned the pot, cover the drainage holes with a mesh – no less than 2mm holes – and place a layer of soil in the bottom. If you are using a suitable soil mix, a drainage course will not be necessary. (f) Make a small mound of soil beneath where the trunk will be and place the tree in position. Gently settle the tree into the mound of soil by rotating slightly back and forth. This will help to stabilize the tree and ensure that the soil penetrates the root mass.

(g) Fill all the remaining space with fresh soil. Use a pencil – or a chopstick if you want to be authentic – to work the soil well in between the roots. Whatever you do, never press the soil down. This will only serve to compact it and will result in poor drainage and all the problems that come with it. Also, there is the possibility that sharp grit in the soil could cause further unnecessary damage to the roots. Leave a gap below the pot's rim to aid watering. (h) It is a good idea to tie the tree into the

(a)

(b)

(c)

(d)

(h)

(e)

(f)

(i)

(g)

pot by passing wire through the drainage holes and up over the roots. This wire can be removed after a month or so, when the new root growth has taken hold.

(i) The newly repotted tree is now ready for another couple of years' healthy growth. Water with a fine spray, taking care not to wash away the loose soil. Place the tree in a sheltered position out of the reach of frost and protected from direct sun and heavy rain until new growth appears.

Bonsai Soils

A good bonsai soil must have three important properties. It must contain sufficient porous, preferably organic, matter to act as a reservoir for water and water-borne nutrients. It must be open enough to allow the unimpeded passage of excess water, and provide sufficient air space to let the roots breathe. And it must be stable enough to hold the tree firmly in its pot.

An ideal mix contains between 20 and 50 per cent leaf mould or peat substitute – the smaller the pot, the greater the proportion. This acts as the reservoir. The remainder of the mix consists of sandy grit. Do not use builder's sand unless it has been weathered for a year or so. Most garden centres sell horticultural sharp sand or alpine grit.

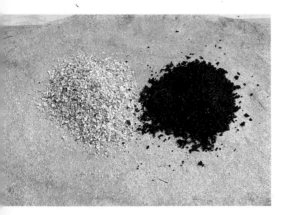

The ingredients of a good bonsai soil mix: equal parts of sandy grit with all the dust sieved out and peat substitute; in this case forest bark which has been sieved to leave particles of around 1–3mm.

If you wish, you can use some inert soil improver such as expanded clay or perlag, so long as it does not replace one of the other ingredients completely. Never use straight-from-the-packet John Innes or other soil-based proprietary composts. They will compact and set like concrete in a short time and are about the worst possible growing medium for bonsai.

All ingredients must be sifted to remove all the large particles and, more importantly all the fine dust. A granular consistency with between 2mm and 4mm particles is perfect. It is not necessary to add any fertilizer to the mix because you will be feeding the tree throughout the growing season anyway.

Pruning

Pruning techniques applied to bonsai are exactly the same as for larger trees but on a much reduced scale, even tree surgeons work on the same principles.

The best time of year to prune any non-flowering tree is spring, just as the buds begin to swell. This minimizes the time before new healing growth takes place. Pines can be pruned in late summer and deciduous trees in autumn, but they will have to survive the rigours of winter before they can begin to heal. Flowering trees should be pruned once they have finished flowering.

Always use sharp tools and cut cleanly. First, remove the branch with secateurs or special branch cutters, and then use a sharp scalpel or modelling knife to carve the stub until it forms a slight hollow. If the stub is too small to work on don't try – it will shrink and fall away after a while, but larger stubs can remain unsightly for years.

Use a wound sealant to protect the cut surfaces from frost and fungal attack. This will also prevent water loss through the wound. Bitumen-based sealants do the job but they are impossible to remove once the wound has healed and they blacken the bark for a long time. If you do not have any special bonsai sealant (*Kyonal*) you can use children's plasticine mixed with a little vegetable oil to prevent it from drying too hard.

Use either a proprietary wound sealant or some DIY mastic compound to protect the wound from frost and water.

Pruning: First prune away the unwanted branch as close to the trunk as possible.

The finished result should be almost invisible and should not detract from the overall appearance of the tree.

Use a sharp modelling knife to clean the wound and to carve the stub flush with the trunk.

Within a few years, the wound will callus over and will create the impression of age.

Larch – *Larix decidua* (Europe) *L. leptolepis* (Japan)
Sources Seeds grow like grass, cuttings can be taken. Few garden centres will stock larch.
A common tree in forestry plantations and in parks and large gardens. One of the few deciduous conifers which adds the extra dimensions of spring and autumn colouring to its charms. The soft needles are normally bright apple green although some trees produce significantly darker foliage.

Summer Pruning

Throughout the growing season you will need to prune away too vigorous shoots and pinch back all the others in order to develop and maintain a neat, tight foliage mass and to create fine twigs. Only your own experience will tell you how often and how much attention each of your trees requires, but as a general principle you should allow it to become a little 'scruffy' and then pinch or

prune back until it is slightly smaller than its ideal shape. In no time at all it will grow back and fill out as the multitude of new shoots spring out.

There are three types of summer pruning techniques which apply in turn to deciduous trees; pines, spruces etc., and junipers and cypresses.

DECIDUOUS TREES

If you want to develop sturdier branches, take the opportunity to prune back to a short spur. This will soon grow longer and will create a better taper and more angular shape.

If you are building foliage masses and twigginess, pinch back the young growth to about two or three leaves. From the point where each leaf joins the shoot (the axil), a new shoot will emerge with smaller leaves and neater growth. By carefully selecting the right place to pinch back to, you can control the direction in which the new shoot

Pinching back young growth to about two or three leaves.

will grow, thereby using simple pinching techniques as a means of shaping future branches.

PINES AND SPRUCES

As these species start to grow in spring, the buds elongate. In the case of spruce they form little tufts, like miniature shaving brushes, while pines form candle-like structures.

The spruce tufts should be broken rather than pinched, removing up to two thirds of

Pine candles should be broken rather than pinched.

New shoots will appear after you have broken spruce tufts.

their length, as soon as they are long enough to get your fingers round. New buds will form at the base of the shoot, and later in the year a few short shoots will appear from the same point. These should not be pinched as they will be needed for next year's growth.

Pine candles should also be broken rather than pinched, leaving about a third behind. Start with the smallest ones and finish with

the larger ones about a week later. New buds will form at the broken point and further back down the branch.

JUNIPERS AND CYPRESSES

There are two types of juniper foliage: needle foliage as with common juniper or Japanese needle juniper; and the cord-like foliage of Chinese Juniper similar to that of cypress. To complicate matters, the cord-like junipers may produce a juvenile foliage consisting of needles. This usually occurs after heavy pruning or root pruning. Shoots bearing this type of foliage should be removed or shortened as soon as they appear.

The technique is the same for both types of foliage. Using your fingers, pinch out the growing tips as soon as they are big enough to handle. Remember that at the base of each needle, or beneath each scale on the cord-like foliage, there is a tiny bud which has the potential to grow into a new shoot.

Bamboo bonsai are difficult to grow but the results can be stunning. This bonsai grove has all the charm and peacefulness of the real thing.

White pine (Pinus parviflora). Three separate trees, none of which are particularly inspiring as individuals, are combined on a rock to produce the most dramatic effect.

The foliage will very soon become so dense that you will have to thin out some shoots periodically to give others room to grow.

Wiring

Although it is possible in some cases to shape a bonsai entirely by pruning, there is always a large element of luck involved and much depends on nature. Only with wiring can you gain almost total control over the shape and form of your tree. Carefully and correctly applied wire can enable you to position exactly each branch, twig and even shoot (if you have the patience). Once you have mastered wiring, which takes only a little practice, the final quality of your bonsai depends only on your artistic ability.

What Wire?

Green plastic-covered garden wire   This is the most readily available type of suitable wire, but only comes in two sizes, and it is a little stiff for our purposes.

Juvenile foliage consisting of needles produced by the cord-like juniper. Remove or shorten these shoots as soon as possible.

Dense foliage means periodical thinning out of shoots.

Copper wire   This type of wire, salvaged from offcuts of electrical cable, furnishes the bonsai grower with a wide range of sizes and at nil cost. It is the best type of wire for conifers and suits most deciduous trees too, although it is still a little stiff for soft shoots or delicate bark.

Aluminium wire   This type, specially made for bonsai use, is the ideal wire for deciduous trees. It is soft and more gentle than the other types but does not have the holding power of either of them. This means that a relatively thick wire is needed to bend any given branch. Aluminium wire is expensive.

Never use uncoated iron or steel wire since it will quickly rust and disfigure the bark and it may even prove fatal to junipers.

(a)

Anchor the wire firmly
by thrusting it into the
soil next to the trunk.

(b)

(c)

Wiring – method

(a) First, anchor the wire firmly. If you are wiring the trunk, push one end of the wire into the soil as close as possible to the trunk. (b) When wiring branches, the wire can be anchored around the base of an adjacent branch or around the trunk itself. (c) Ideally, you should use one piece of wire for two adjacent branches. This minimizes the potential damage to the bark and provides a perfect anchorage. (d) Spiral the wire around the branch or trunk at roughly a 45 degree angle. If the wire is too loose it will not hold the branch in position; too tight and it will disfigure the bark. Gentle contact is all that is needed. (e) If one piece of wire is not sufficient to hold the branch in place, you can apply another alongside it. On no account spiral it in the opposite direction, or the pressure caused at the points where the wires cross will seriously damage the bark.

(f) Remember that it is just as easy to damage the tree when you remove the wire as it is when you apply it. For this reason, it is best to cut the wire away with sharp wire cutters of the type which cut right up to the tip. I know this seems wasteful, but ask yourself which is worth more – the wire or the tree.

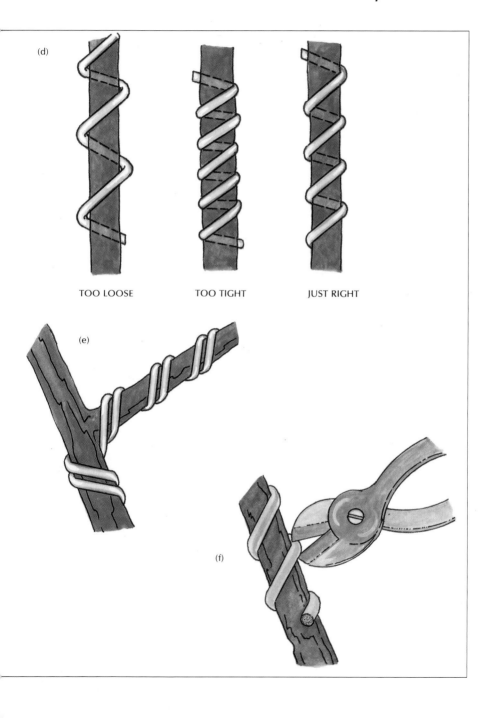

(d)

TOO LOOSE TOO TIGHT JUST RIGHT

(e)

(f)

Wire should be removed before it begins to cut into the bark.

Before you wire, test the pliability of the branch against that of the wire. With a little practice you will be able to judge surprisingly accurately the right thickness for each branch.

Wire should be removed before it begins to cut into the bark as growth takes place. Watch the top of the tree especially, as this is where the branches will thicken first. Wire damage can take years, even decades to grow out.

Watering

Watering is largely a matter of common sense coupled with careful observation of your trees. While no pot must ever be allowed to dry out, since this will probably kill the tree, no pot should ever become waterlogged either. The consequences of waterlogging may not be so sudden but can be equally damaging in the long run. Waterlogged roots will not be able to breathe and will begin to rot within a short time. Once this process has begun, it is sometimes difficult to stop it. This is why a free draining soil is so important.

In winter you will only need to check the soil for dryness every week or two and you may not need to actually water for months. But as spring approaches and the tree begins to take up more water, the soil will start to dry out. This process can begin quite suddenly, so keep an eye open.

As growth increases and the weather warms up, the water requirements of your trees also increases and you may find yourself watering once or even twice a day. If the soil surface is still slightly moist, then there is still an adequate moisture content,

Yew – *Taxus baccata* (Europe)
Sources Self-sown seedlings are common in the vicinity of mature plants. Garden centres will stock several varieties.
Rich, dark green needles contrasting with bright red berries make yew a most attractive tree. It is very slow growing but can live for up to a thousand years!

Zelkova Serrata, broom style. *The technique described on page 29 was employed to start this tree's development many years ago. Since then, constant pruning and pinching each year has produced this beautiful fine tracery of twigs.*

but if it is bone dry, then it is probably time to water. Experience will help you judge more accurately, but in the beginning you can scratch away a little soil at the edge of the pot to inspect a little deeper. Don't do this too often though or you may damage young roots. Sometimes, you may find that the wind has dried out the surface completely but the soil below is still quite moist.

Water from above using a watering can with a fine rose or a fine spray on a hose at low power. Water the pot thoroughly, filling the space between the surface of the soil and the rim of the pot. Wait until that has soaked in and repeat. You should by then see water draining through the holes in the bottom of the pot, which indicates a good watering and proper drainage. If this does not happen, then perhaps your soil is not draining properly. Lift the tree gently out of the pot and see if the water has penetrated the soil. If so, then fine; if not,

take extra care over watering and change your soil mix next spring.

Feeding

All a bonsai really needs to keep it healthy is a good balanced feed intended for use with container-grown plants. There are many available on the market and the big name brands are as good as any. Read the instructions carefully and whatever you do, don't exceed the stated dosage, you certainly won't be doing your tree a favour. You will achieve better results if you use a quarter-strength solution at every watering, since this ensures a constant supply of nutrients in adequate quantities for a tree.

Start feeding once new growth is well under way, not before. The idea is to feed according to the tree's current need, not its future needs. Carry on feeding regularly

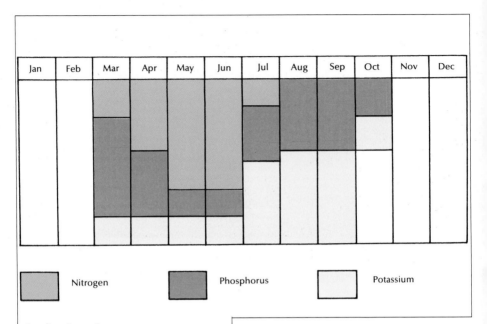

Jan	Feb	Mar	Apr	May	Jun	Jul	Aug	Sep	Oct	Nov	Dec

Nitrogen   Phosphorus   Potassium

Feeding Bonsai

The three main elements in plant nutrition are: Nitrogen (responsible for leaf and shoot growth), Phosphorus (roots) and Potassium (ripening growth and inducing flowering) – known chemically as N, P, and K respectively.

Since your plants' requirements differ according to the season, your bonsai will be a lot healthier and happier if you can also adjust the proportions of each of these main elements accordingly. Take care not to overfeed and ensure that you give your plant sufficient trace elements – the trace element content of most fertilizers can be found on the packet.

The accompanying table illustrates the ideal proportions of N, P and K throughout the growing season.

to bring about specific effects. For example, if a tree has suffered a recent root problem or is slow to develop new roots, a fertilizer high in phosphorus (P) and low in nitrogen (N) will boost root growth.

A fruiting or flowering tree performs better on a diet containing a higher than normal amount of potassium (K). Potassium also helps to ripen current year's growth in preparation for winter, so a late season dose of a high P and K feed is a good idea around late August and September.

Where rapid top growth is required, a high nitrogen (N) fertilizer should be employed, but in dilute amounts. This will produce vigorous shoots which may be used for creating new branches quickly. It also increases the intensity of the colour of the leaves. Never apply high nitrogen feeds after mid-summer. The effect will persist until late in the year and will result in weak sappy autumn shoots which will not survive the winter.

until mid-summer and then begin to reduce the amount and frequency until early autumn when you should stop altogether.

More sophisticated feeding regimes employing specialist fertilizers can be used

One note of caution. Underfeeding may eventually kill a tree after many years, but overfeeding can do it almost overnight in some cases.

Jins and Sharis

Translated literally the word *Jin* means Godhead. In bonsai terms it is a branch or apex of the trunk which has had the bark stripped away, has been shaped and finally bleached in order to imitate the storm-battered deadwood on ancient mountain pines. So it is easier to stick to the term jin! A *shari* is a similarly treated strip of exposed wood running the length of the trunk.

The object of jins and sharis is to enhance the aged appearance of coniferous bonsai and they are often employed as a means of disguising an awkward wound or terminating a trunk without causing a large scar.

Begin by peeling away the bark with a sharp scalpel or modelling knife. Cut right back to the trunk so the jin appears to be growing out of a hole in the bark. This hole will heal and fill in a short time but will not cause a swelling around the jin which would happen otherwise.

Next, crush the end of the branch stub with pliers and peel back small strips of wood. This exposes the grain and creates a naturally shaped taper. Carving with a knife cannot produce the same effect.

*Needle juniper (*Juniperus rigida*). This semi-cascade was originally created by utilizing only the lowest branch of what was a much larger tree.*

A tiny Japanese needle juniper (Juniperus rigida) *measuring no more than 8in (20cm) in height.*

When you are happy with the shape, you can bleach and preserve the wood with lime sulphur solution (available through most bonsai retailers) or with clear, horticultural wood preserver mixed with white poster paint. The former is by far the most satisfactory, but more difficult to obtain.

The creation of jins and sharis is an art form in itself and preoccupies some bonsai artists more than the living part of the tree. Massive chunks of deadwood are carved into fantastic shapes using chain saws, power-chisels and die-grinders as well as a whole host of custom-built tools. The results are stunning, very heavy and very, very expensive masterpieces.

5 • STYLING YOUR BONSAI

Regardless of the raw material you are working with, be it a seedling, garden centre plant or a giant from the shrubbery, the principles of styling are the same. In essence, your aim is to create in miniature an illusion of a fully-grown tree. You may choose the image of a massive broom style elm standing in an open field, or perhaps a tortured pine clinging to life on an exposed mountain top. So long as the chosen style is suitable for the species in question, then your imagination can take over.

Before you start, spend some time just looking at the trees around you. Notice how all the growth points away from the centre of the tree, each branch filling the nearest space, and how the branches become thinner towards the top. With the knowledge you have already gained of how trees grow from season to season, you should now be able to work out how the shapes of branches on full-sized trees were formed.

You will begin to see how age also affects the shapes of trees. How, as they grow older, their branches begin to droop as they are weighted down by foliage and snow over the years. Lower branches die off in some species, producing a tall literati style; in others, age manifests itself in a tremendous thickening of the trunk and main limbs, producing a short, heavy, informal upright style.

Now you are ready to apply your newly acquired techniques, your knowledge of trees and your artistic skills to the business of creating a bonsai.

The most effective way to explain the progression of styling a bonsai is to show you. The species I chose for the sequence of photographs is a common juniper (*Juniperus communis*) – one of the several dwarf varieties readily available. Junipers are tough plants and pot-grown specimens allow you to prune, wire and root prune all in one session provided you do the work mid-spring and can provide sheltered, humid conditions for a few weeks afterwards. Even

so, if I had not been styling the tree for demonstration purposes I would have waited a year before repotting.

The first thing to decide upon is the 'front' or the preferred viewing angle. It may be that the root formation is better one side than the other, or the trunk line is more dramatic when viewed from a certain angle. In the case of the juniper it was the fact that it offered two trunks which influenced this decision.

Step by Step

(a) A fairly nondescript and rather mangy looking juniper. This is fairly typical of the type of plant you find being sold off cheaply by garden centres. Its loss of foliage at the base has made it undesirable as a garden plant, but as a bonsai . . .

(b)

(c)

(d)

(b) The plant is removed from its pot and the surface roots are exposed. Also, since whatever style is eventually chosen the tree will need a trunk, some of the lowest branches are removed. At this point the style becomes obvious: one of the lowest branches actually forms a second trunk. The 'mother and child' image of a large and small tree growing together is one of my favourites.

(c) Now the right way round, more branches are removed as the image of an ancient pine begins to emerge. Some wire is applied to the trunk and a gentle nodding curve is introduced to give the composition energy.

(d) More pruning and wiring, this time on the smaller trunk. A subsidiary trunk like this, on a full-sized tree, will always bend out towards the light. Somehow this sudden change in direction is a little harsh for the style I have in mind. It needs altering.

(e)

(f)

(g)

(e)   That's better. I have also wired the branches on the small trunk and positioned them more or less to my satisfaction. See how the branches tend to fall away from the trunk and then level out to form more or less horizontal pads of foliage.

(f)   This trunk now has only three branches and the foliage has been thinned drastically. Masses of buds will now form all along the branches and twigs. Any that grow downwards must be removed and all others shortened to a few sets of needles.

(g)   There are still a lot of unwanted branches at the top of the main trunk. By holding down a couple at a time you can begin to get an idea of which to put where.

(h)   The decision is made and the bottom two branches are positioned with wire. Note the branch pointing to the rear. It is essential to have back branches in order to give the composition depth. The foliage is thinned as it was on the small trunk's

(h)

(i)

(j)

branches. Again, all downward-pointing growth is cut away to expose the embryonic branch structure.

(i) The process of wiring and pruning continues on an ever-diminishing scale right to the apex of the tree. Care is taken not to clutter up the top of the tree with too many small branches, as this is the area where growth will be most vigorous so it will fill out very soon. In fact, the top will need to be thinned at regular yearly intervals in future, whereas the lower branches will only require this treatment every three years or so. But I stress again: keep all branches free of downward-pointing shoots. It is also important to remember not to have any branch growing directly above another as this will shade and weaken the one below. Also, no branch should be allowed to grow directly opposite another as this causes a jar to the eye and makes the composition look awkward.

(j) After completion, the bonsai is root pruned and repotted as described in Chapter 4. The wire will be left on until it becomes so tight that it may damage the bark. It will then be cut away and if necessary re-applied. It may take several applications of wire over many years before the thicker branches have set on this particular species but the work will be rewarded in the long run.

This type of 'instant bonsai' is only possible with plants which have small, densely packed foliage like juniper, dwarf spruces, or cypress. With other species, particularly deciduous trees, the process can take a few years, growing on branches where no suitably placed one could be found. Sometimes the initial styling will merely consist of

The same hawthorn two years later. The mass of new shoots provides ample opportunity for creating new branches when initial training begins next spring.

This hawthorn, now only 1ft (30cm) tall, was originally nearly 6ft (1.8m) tall when it was collected from a neighbour's front hedge. Almost all the branches have been removed and the tree has been tied into its training pot (an old washing-up bowl with drainage holes added). It will be left undisturbed for two years in order to build up a healthy root system before training can begin.

pruning away all but a few stubs, leaving just the basic trunk and main limbs, and waiting for new growth to establish before moving on to the next stage.

When styling young seedlings or cuttings you have the advantage of being able to determine the exact trunk shape as well as the eventual size and form of the tree. This total control, if exercised properly, can compensate for the many years of waiting

Pines – *Pinus* spp. (Widely distributed)
Sources Seed, self-sown seedlings of indigenous varieties; garden centres sell some dwarf varieties as well as fairly large plants intended for large gardens. Japanese white pine (*P. parviflora*) is available from all bonsai nurseries.

This larch, now eight years old, was grown from seed collected in the Welsh mountains.

for the bark to take on the naturally occurring fissures and cracks which depict age and which can already be present on larger raw material.

Care must be taken not to be too enthusiastic about introducing wild and fantastic shapes in the trunk. Instead, try to make the line interesting without being un-tree-like.

Always keep in mind the eventual size and style of the image you intend to create. If possible, try to draw it and decide where you would ideally like the branches to form. Keep this drawing and refer to it each time you work on the tree. Obviously as time goes by you will make changes to the design, and adapt it to the plant's particular growth pattern, but it is an invaluable exercise, especially for the beginner.

A newly rooted cutting of cotoneaster microphylla *which has been wired into a cascade style. At this stage, all you see are the bare bones of the bonsai; it will appear quite differently in a few years' time.*

Once you have established the branches, you can resort to a regime of prune, prune and prune again, with the occasional thinning back of overcrowded growth and the odd bit of wiring here and there. Photograph your trees each year at least once and keep the pictures for reference. You may not notice the changes in your trees on a day-to-day basis but when you look back at photographs taken over the years the transformation can be dramatic and this can be a tremendous eye-opener.

6 • THE BONSAI CALENDAR

Although spring is by far the busiest time of the bonsai year there is always something that needs doing. Of course, the exact month in which you carry out certain tasks will depend on where you live. The arrival of spring in the north of Scotland can be up to six weeks later than in the south of England. Your trees will tell you, for example, when they are ready for spring by putting a shine on their swelling buds.

So combine the following monthly work-list with your own observation and ever-increasing experience.

January

Below ground Do not repot or root prune. Small trees may be eased from their pots and have their roots immersed in moist peat during the really cold weather.

Above ground No wiring or pruning. Any wounds will have to wait for months before they can heal, so don't take the risk.

General Check all trees under shelter every week for drought or winter pests such as spruce aphid or spider mite. Do not allow pots kept outside to become waterlogged – this causes more deaths than freezing. During prolonged spells of below-freezing temperatures, trees should be protected from drying winds, since the needles and buds can still lose moisture but the roots cannot absorb it. Prepare your tools and soils for spring; photograph your collection.

February

Below ground Tough deciduous trees like hawthorn or English elm can be repotted towards the end of the month if you can keep them free from very severe frosts afterwards. Maples, fruiting and flowering species, and more tender plants should be left for a month.

Above ground Towards the end of the month, if the weather is mild, you can undertake light trimming of last year's shoots on hardy deciduous trees. Don't wire just yet, and save the hard pruning until later.

General Some trees may be starting to take in water so be vigilant. Plan your future designs with sketches and photos. At this time of year many trees, both deciduous and coniferous, begin to stir at the root tips and the buds begin to swell very slightly. Don't be fooled into thinking spring is here! It can take another month or two for proper growth to begin.

March

Below ground You can start repotting early this month. Begin with native deciduous trees, then with imports. Finish with spruces. Save other conifers until next month. Keep all newly repotted trees relatively free from frost until new growth is obvious. Avoid allowing too much rain to waterlog repotted trees.

Above ground Prune away, beginning with deciduous trees any time from the middle of the month. Seal all wounds against frost and moisture loss. Light pruning back to conveniently located swelling buds can set your tree on course for the imminent growing season. As some early species leaf out, they will start to require more water and will become prone to aphid attack, so keep on your guard.

Remove old wire and wait for a few weeks to see if the branches are fully set.

General This is the busiest time of year. For the next two months you will be carrying out almost every bonsai technique in the book so don't plan any holidays. Check pots daily for moisture and pests.

Pests and Diseases

Bonsai are no more prone to pests and diseases than any other plant but because they are confined in small pots and their growth rate is slow, they are not able to outgrow an attack of aphids or powdery mildew as efficiently as free-range plants. Always take remedial action as soon as you spot the trouble – using a proprietary insecticide or fungicide and following the manufacturer's instructions exactly. Very few maladies will actually kill a bonsai but they will quickly disfigure it and may even cause it to lose a branch or two.

The most serious disease is root-rot, and because it is below the soil it is impossible to spot until it has already taken hold. The symptoms are general lack of vigour, wilting and occasionally distorted leaves. This is followed by yellowing and falling leaves, and eventually death. The best cure is prevention, by ensuring good drainage in the pot, but if one of your trees does suffer root-rot do the following without delay:

Immediately ease the tree from the pot and allow all the dead roots to fall away. Do not try to force them away from the soil mass – if they don't fall, leave them. Remove any soil which clearly does not contain any roots. Place the tree in a large *well drained* container with a layer of grit in the bottom and fill with a mixture of 80 per cent grit and 20 per cent peat. Leave for at least one year before disturbing.

root-rot

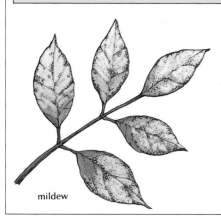

mildew

aphids

Tidy the soil surface of trees not due for repotting. This is a good time to dig up plants from the open ground. Make sure you have an appropriate container and plenty of bonsai soil at hand.

April

Below ground Finish repotting deciduous and coniferous trees by the end of this month.

Above ground Wiring may now begin on deciduous trees but one word of warning: take care not to knock off any fragile swelling buds as you work; they are *very* easy to dislodge at this stage. Carry on pruning deciduous trees, making sure that the branches you leave are alive and healthy.

As the month progresses, you can become more drastic in your pruning and wiring, as you grow in confidence and your trees grow in strength.

General Any trees which have not yet stirred should be placed in a humid and shaded frost-free environment such as a polytunnel. It is not unknown for an ailing tree to wait until July before leafing out, so be patient.

Your watering regime will start in earnest around now, as the warmer weather and the new growth place increased demands on the pot's water-holding capacity. Give the first feed to trees which either have not been repotted or which were repotted more than four weeks ago.

May

Below ground Finish repotting conifers you didn't get round to last month. Root growth will now be vigorous on deciduous species so they should not be disturbed except in dire circumstances, in which case they should be placed in a polytunnel or similar for a month or so afterwards.

Above ground Early species will begin to require pinching of the shoot tips to maintain outline and encourage bushy growth. Unwanted shoots and buds should be removed.

By the end of May your deciduous trees will have filled out a lot and you will then be able to revise the design of the branches accordingly by pruning and wiring. Don't do conifers just yet.

General Nature is really on the move now – including all the pests and diseases. Treat all infestations as soon as they are noticed with dilute garden pesticides and fungicides. Feeding may also now begin in earnest.

Water as frequently as your trees demand – perhaps twice a day if small pots are exposed to the warm sun and the wind.

Check on early wiring in case it is beginning to cut into the swelling bark.

June

Below ground No repotting except for Chinese junipers which can be given the benefit of a polytunnel, and then only gentle root pruning.

Above ground Pine candles and spruce shoots will need to be pinched back early in June. Deciduous trees will need constant pinching to keep them in trim.

Wire conifers and deciduous trees once the first flush of growth has set, which for pines will not be until towards the end of the month.

Vigorous deciduous trees may be defoliated towards the end of the month in order to increase twigginess, but do not do this on young trees in training since it will retard their growth and delay their development.

General Constant watering and careful checking for disease and general health are the main tasks this month. Wire applied earlier in the year may now have served its purpose and may be harming the tree, so inspect this daily. Feed well.

July

Below ground Leave alone.

Above ground Spray in the evening in hot weather, your trees will appreciate a cool shower as much as you! Pruning and wiring can be carried out to good effect on all trees. A considerable amount of greenery can be removed in the early part of the month as there is still plenty of time for regrowth.
Keep pinching out new growth.

General Begin to reduce the nitrogen in the fertilizer this month. Continue the daily regime of watering and inspection for problems such as aphids or tightening wires. Some sensitive trees (maples, hornbeams, for example) will need some kind of shading from the hot sun to prevent leaf scorch. Remove old needles from pines and spruces, and pinch out new growing tips on Chinese junipers in particular.

August

Below ground Leave alone.

Above ground This is a good time for pruning pines and for creating jins and sharis if you can afford the trees some shelter for a week or so. The wounds will dry quickly and there is still time for rapid healing. Pruning deciduous trees at this time may cause die-back of the rest of the branch in question if the tree can channel its energies elsewhere, so this is best avoided at this time. Wiring can be carried out.

General Growth begins to slow down now, so reduce the nitrogen in the fertilizer to nil. Pinching of all species except Chinese junipers and cypresses will also become increasingly less necessary as the month progresses. Water uptake will still be high so keep up the daily regime. Tidy up the inner branches of crowded conifers by removing old brown needles and thinning out where necessary.

September

Below ground Autumn repotting of conifers may start towards the end of the month but only with a minimum of root pruning.

Above ground No wiring except perhaps gentle tinkering on pines and spruces and on Chinese junipers. Do not prune now, as it may result in a late surge of growth which could weaken the tree and will be prone to destruction by the first frosts of autumn.

General A last feed of nitrogen-free fertilizer may be given this month. Be careful not to overwater as the tree's requirements decrease. Trunks and branches fatten rapidly at this time of year so wires can begin to cut into the bark within days. Check daily for this and for signs of late insect attack. A diet of moderate watering, sunny days and cold nights will help promote vivid autumn colours.

October

Below ground Conifers may be repotted now. Deciduous trees only if they are already in autumn colour. Take special care to keep autumn-repotted trees free of hard frost all winter.

A formal upright English elm grown from a cutting in five years.

Above ground Autumn pruning can take place if deciduous trees have lost their leaves and if pines are strong. Seal all wounds thoroughly as they will have to endure the winter before they can heal properly. There is no point in wiring now since there will be no growth until next year and the wire will have little or no effect.

General Remove dead leaves from the pot and from the branches if they get caught there. This will reduce the likelihood of decay or insect attack. Good hygiene is important at this time of year because the tree is now losing its ability to combat pests and diseases by outgrowing them. In spite of the lack of growth pots may still dry out with surprising rapidity.

November

Below ground Finish autumn repotting this month, but remember that you can't be as drastic now as you can in the spring. The roots will have to wait until spring before they can regenerate and this leaves plenty of time for decay to set in. Species with fleshy roots, such as trident maples and chinese elms are particularly susceptible to root rot following winter repotting.

Above ground Keep cleaning away dead leaves and other debris. Prune deciduous or coniferous trees except Chinese junipers. Their season runs late and they may still put on a surge of growth which would be snapped off by hard frost. Don't wire this month as winter frosts and winds may enter the tiny cracks that will occur in the bark, and this may cause the entire branch to die back.

General Prepare your winter protection now. A sheet of polythene draped over the benches, forming a tent, is an easy and effective way to keep the worst of the winter weather off your bonsai. Your trees will live quite happily under there all winter but inspect them every week for signs of dryness or insect attack. Most Novembers are mild enough for all trees to stay outside, but it is worth preparing for a sudden very cold snap – it happens when you least expect it!

December

Below ground No activity except in emergencies. Keep any root damage to an

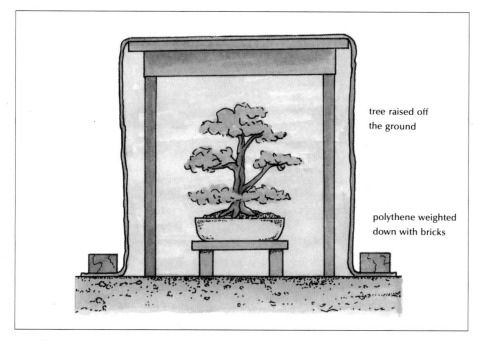

tree raised off
the ground

polythene weighted
down with bricks

A small tree embedded in a box of peat. This serves to insulate the roots and provides good winter protection.

absolute minimum and protect the tree from frost for the remainder of the winter.

Above ground No wiring or pruning unless avoidable. If you must prune in December use a thick coating of wound sealant to protect the damaged tissues from frost and fungal attack. Spray with a winter wash to kill insect eggs and larvae. A spray of dilute fungicide will also help protect your tree during the cold months ahead.

General Place all small or slightly tender trees in their winter quarters. Small trees can be embedded in boxes of peat in order to further insulate the roots but remove all moss first. The insects and larvae which live naturally in the moss will be more active in these conditions and may harm the tree's roots. Leave pines out on the benches unless

the weather becomes extremely cold. Larger deciduous trees should be placed in a sheltered spot, protected from the wind.

Finish cleaning away all dead leaves and debris which could harbour insects or fungal spores. Tidy around the benches, removing old pruning debris and replacing any decaying wood.

Make a Christmas list of any tools, pots, books or other equipment you need. Take your time when selecting pots, and if possible take the tree along to the stockist so you can try different pots for size and colour etc.

This is also a good time to bring your records up to date by cataloguing photographs and organizing notes. Look back over previous years and compare the success rates of fertilizers and watering practices etc. Look forward to next year and make notes about your future plans for each tree.

GLOSSARY

Adventitious Applies to shoots which emerge from parts of the plant other than the growing points.

Aerial roots Roots which grow from parts of a plant which are above the soil level.

Alternate Describes the pattern of leaves which grow singly at different levels on a shoot (*see* opposite).

Apex The extreme growing point of a branch, or more normally a trunk.

Axil The angle between a leaf stem and its parent shoot. Leaf axils contain a bud from which future growth can emerge.

Bankan A style of bonsai with a twisted or spiral trunk.

Bole The clear part of a trunk, from ground level to the first branch.

Broad-leaved Applies to any tree except conifers.

Broom A bonsai style based on the natural growth habit of *Zelkova serrata*.

Bud A tightly packed embryonic shoot usually encased in scales which are themselves modified leaves.

Bunjingi Bonsai style otherwise known as *Literati*.

Callus The healing 'scar' tissue which forms around a wound and eventually grows over it.

Cambium The thin layer of actively growing tissue between the bark and the heartwood. Throughout the growing season this layer continually produces new bark on the outside and new heartwood on the inside thus increasing the girth and creating the annual rings.

Chokkan Formal upright style bonsai. The trunk must be dead straight right to the apex of the tree.

Compost Decaying or decayed vegetable matter. The term is also often used to describe other inert growing media.

Conifer A cone-bearing tree usually, but not always, with needle-like foliage.

Cotyledon The first two (or more) 'seed leaves' which emerge from the seed shell.

Crown The upper and outer foliage-bearing branches.

Damping-off A fungal disease caused by waterlogged or poorly ventilated conditions which causes seedlings to collapse and die.

Deciduous Describes a tree or shrub which loses its leaves at the end of each growing season.

Defoliation The removal of all leaves. This is sometimes carried out on deciduous trees to encourage the production of new leaves and finer twigs.

Die-back The withering and drying out of shoots, twigs and even whole branches. Among the many possible causes are underwatering, disease, poor rootage and exposure to strong sun or wind.

Dormant Bud A bud which failed to produce growth during the first year following its formation but which remains viable for several years.

Dormant Period The tree's resting period, usually during winter, when it puts on little or no growth, and when deciduous trees are leafless.

Driftwood The *sharimiki* style of bonsai, with much exposed deadwood on the trunk and branches.

Dwarf A genetic mutation of a species, which grows more slowly and is more compact.

Evergreen A tree or shrub which bears its leaves throughout the year.

Flush A period of rapid growth. Most trees produce a flush in spring and under good conditions will produce a second flush in June or July.

Fluted Describes the shape of a trunk which has vertical rounded grooves running from the roots upwards.

Fukinagashi The windswept style of bonsai.

Girth The thickness of a trunk measured at the lowest point possible above the root spread.

Go-kan Bonsai style with five trunks.

Habit The natural shape or growth pattern of a plant.

Han-kengai Semi-cascade style of bonsai.

Hardwood An alternative term for deciduous trees.

Hardy Describes a plant which can survive outdoors during the winter in northern Europe due to its ability to tolerate freezing temperatures for long periods.

Hokidachi Japanese term for *broom* style bonsai.

Humus Partially decayed vegetable matter present in the soil.

Ikadabuki Raft-style bonsai, created by laying the trunk on the soil and training the branches upwards to form new 'trunks'. Roots develop along the underside of the horizontal trunk.

Internode The distance between the nodes or leaf axils on a shoot.

Jin A branch or trunk apex which has had its bark removed and has been bleached and shaped to represent damage by lightning or harsh winds etc.

Kabaduchi Clump style bonsai formed by cutting a trunk back to ground level and training the many new shoots which emerge into new trunks.

Kengai Cascade style bonsai.

Lateral A shoot which emerges from a bud on a main shoot or stem.

Leader The main vertical stem or shoot of a young plant.

Lime sulphur A compound used for bleaching and preserving *jins* or *sharis*.

Mame Miniature bonsai. The generally accepted maximum size for mame bonsai is six inches.

Moyogi Informal upright style of bonsai.

Neagari Exposed root style of bonsai.

Nebari The visible parts of the roots of a tree as they radiate from the trunk.

Netsunanari Root-connected style bonsai. The individual trunks, which may be trained in any style, are all growing from the same root system although not connected in any other way.

Node A stem joint or the point to which a leaf or leaves are attached.

Opposite The arrangement of leaves in pairs along either side of the shoot.

Organic Any chemical compound containing carbon. In horticultural terms describes a growing technique free from artificial chemically-based fertilizers or pesticides etc.

Petiole Leaf stalk or stem.

pH The acid/alkaline balance of a growing medium. A pH of more than 7.5 is likely to be too alkaline for most plants and one below 6 too acid.

Photosynthesis The process by which a plant converts water and carbon dioxide into sugars with the aid of the chlorophyll in the leaves combined with sunlight.

Respiration The action of exchanging carbon dioxide from the plant with oxygen from the atmosphere during the process of releasing stored foodstuffs.

Sapwood The living wood which is located between the heartwood and the *cambium* layer.

Sekijoju Root-over-rock style bonsai.

Shakan Slanting style bonsai.

Sharimiki A part of the trunk which has had the bark removed and the exposed wood has been bleached.

Sokan Double or twin-trunk style bonsai.

Spur A short lateral growth which extends only very little each year and usually carries flower buds.

Tender Describes any plant which will not tolerate temperatures of 0°C or lower.

Terminal The uppermost shoot, flower or bud.

Transpiration The continual loss of water through the surfaces of the leaves and stems.

Variety A variation of a species which may occur naturally or as the result of human intervention.

Vegetative Describes propagation by means other than seed.

Yôse-ue Group or multi-trunk style bonsai.

INDEX